Kongo and Kumba
TWO GORILLAS

Kongo and Kumba
TWO GORILLAS

by Alice Schick

pictures by Joseph Cellini

THE DIAL PRESS NEW YORK

Library of Congress Cataloging in Publication Data
Schick, Alice. Kongo and Kumba: two gorillas.
Summary: Describes the first three years of one gorilla cared
for by its mother in the wild and of another cared for by a zoo.
1. Gorillas—Juvenile literature. 2. Zoo animals—Juvenile literature.
[1. Gorillas. 2. Zoo animals] I. Cellini, Joseph, illus. II. Title.
QL737.P96S34   599.884   74–2397
ISBN 0–8037–4613–X   lib. 0–8037–4619–9

1812417

for Joel

This book could not have been written without the kindness and cooperation of the staff and volunteers at Lincoln Park Zoo. I would particularly like to thank Lester Fisher, D.V.M., Saul Kitchener, Carl Kleeberger, Tony Martinez, Jim Higgins, Pat Sass, and Dorothy Brunken. And of course, special thanks go to George Schaller and Dian Fossey, whose superb field studies of gorillas made the story of Kongo possible.

Foreword

It was a precious moment for a zoo director—the opportunity to witness the birth of the Lincoln Park Zoo's first baby gorilla. At 6:00 P.M. on July 22, 1970, Kumba was born.

The first captive birth of a gorilla took place in 1956 in Columbus, Ohio. Since then births have been increasing throughout the zoo world. Better husbandry, diets and general care of the animals in the collection reflect the growing concern of zoos for all wildlife.

In the coming years gorillas, an endangered species, could disappear from their homes in the wild and their survival as a species may depend on the available captive stock.

Man can learn much about himself from studies of animals, and this is especially true of observations on the great apes. Therefore, the captive propagation of all rare and endangered species is a prized goal of every zoo administrator.

Alice Schick has combined careful research and lively writing in her account of the first three years in the lives of a wild gorilla and a zoo gorilla. Her book is both an engrossing study of animal behavior and a look at the directions in which modern zoos are moving in the care of our precious wildlife.

L. E. Fisher, D.V.M.
Zoological Gardens Director
Lincoln Park Zoo

Kongo and Kumba
TWO GORILLAS

Kongo
YEAR ONE

Deep inside Central Africa lies a chain of eight tall mountains. Two of the Virunga Mountains are active volcanoes. Not many animals live there, and the plants are few and tough. The other six mountains are volcanoes too. But they no longer erupt. On these mountains the rich volcanic soil and the moist air have produced thick green jungles of plant life. Many animals make their homes in

3

the mountain jungles—buffaloes, antelope, elephants, leopards. There too live some of the last of the wild gorillas.

One morning a group of seventeen mountain gorillas sat feeding on a mountain slope. The warm sun had chased the cold mists of night and dried the animals' gleaming black fur. There was more than enough food—wild celery, Galium vines, thistles, berries, and leaves—to satisfy the largest gorilla appetite. Even the leader of the group, an enormous male with silver fur on his back, was relaxed and content.

Suddenly an eight-year-old female dropped the stalk of wild celery she held and stood up. A look of pain came into her gentle brown eyes. She looked around the group. Then she turned and hurried out of the clearing.

For twenty minutes the rest of the group could not see or hear her. They continued to feed slowly and happily without seeming to notice her disappearance.

Just as suddenly as she had left, the young female returned. She walked awkwardly on both feet and the knuckles of one hand. In her other arm she cradled her newborn infant.

The two-hundred-pound gorilla mother had just given birth to her first baby—a tiny four-pound creature. Like all newborn gorillas, the infant was totally helpless.

4

It was too weak even to hold on to the mother's fur. It was so small and so still that if the young mother had not seen newborn infants with other mothers in the group, she might not have recognized her own baby as a living thing that needed her care.

But observation of many mothers and babies had taught the young mother what to do. With her hands and tongue she cleaned and dried the little gorilla. She helped the tiny mouth to find a nipple, and the newborn ape began to nurse. The new mother seemed tired but happy. Fondly she watched her child as she tore at a handful of leaves to continue her own interrupted meal.

Gorillas, like other animals, have no need for names. Much of their communication is soundless. But if the young gorilla mother had named her new son, she might have called him Kongo, which was the name of an ancient African kingdom.

The group had been feeding for more than two hours. Most of the animals had had enough to eat. Now it was time to rest. The huge silverback leaned against a tree trunk. Two females slowly walked toward him on the soles of their feet and the knuckles of their hands and sat down. They seemed to want to be near the leader, not because they were afraid of anything, but because they liked him. Several of the adult gorillas lay down on the ground, rolling onto their backs, stomachs, or sides—whichever position seemed most comfortable. Some animals dozed in the warm sun.

One young gorilla climbed a small tree. When he reached a place where two branches formed a V, he began to build a nest. He pulled a number of branches in and crushed them under his feet to make a platform. Then he packed down the branches and broke off any twigs that stuck out. He used the broken ends to build a rim. The young gorilla lay down in his day nest with his head on his hands and his legs crossed at the knees. He looked as if he were thinking serious but pleasant thoughts.

A few of the gorillas used the rest period to groom themselves. They scratched their heads and carefully inspected the hair and skin on their arms and legs. Two young animals groomed each other. One mother tried hard to groom her year-old infant, but the child refused to sit still. It squirmed about, trying to get away from the mother to join three larger youngsters who were playing a game that looked very much like tag.

The new mother hardly saw any of these things. She was completely absorbed in her baby. She sat very still, holding Kongo in her arms. She couldn't take her eyes off him. The baby was quiet. He did not cry or make noise. But now and then he stirred. When he moved, the mother rocked him gently until he fell back to sleep.

The rest period lasted about two hours. The silver-back stood up and stretched. He began to walk off into the forest. Quickly the rest of the group prepared to leave. The juvenile left his nest in the tree. Mothers gathered up unruly infants. The younger children rode on their mothers' backs while larger children scrambled to keep up with the group.

The gorillas moved slowly through the thick forest, making frequent stops to eat. An animal did not have to move far in the dense vegetation to be hidden from the others. When the group scattered too far, the silverback called them softly and the gorillas moved on.

In three hours of walking the gorillas covered less than half a mile. The pace was slow enough so that the new mother carrying the still-helpless infant could easily keep up. At the age of eight hours Kongo had started to make clutching motions at his mother's fur. But he was still far too weak to hold on without her help.

By late afternoon the gorillas were ready to begin settling down for the night. They did not look for a place where they had slept before or make an attempt to find the ideal sleeping place—almost any spot in the forest was fine. Around dusk the gorillas began to settle down wherever they happened to be.

All the animals began to move very slowly, even more slowly than usual. The group collected around the

7

silverback. Most of the gorillas just sat waiting for their leader to make the next move. The newborn stirred in his mother's arms, and she used the quiet time to nurse him once again.

After a while the silverback stood up and walked over to an inviting clump of vegetation. Slowly and deliberately he began to snap branches for his nest. Soon the other animals began to move off to build nests of their own.

Although they rarely built sleeping nests during the day, all the gorillas in the group made nests at night. The silverback leader always built his nest on the ground. He was too heavy to feel really comfortable in the trees. Many of the younger animals and most of the females chose nearby trees for their nests. Only the infants of the group did not build nests of their own but slept with their mothers.

The new mother chose a low tree within sight of the silverback for her nest. Gorilla nests are usually simple and not very elegant, but her nest was messier than usual on this day. She did not put down her baby even while she built the nest, and she had not yet perfected a one-handed technique.

Once the gorillas had finished their nests, they wasted no time in getting down to the serious business of sleeping. By the time the sun had set and darkness and

cold had crept over the forest, the eighteen gorillas were quiet. The new mother slept soundly with her baby in her arms.

The next day was much the same for the gorillas—a leisurely awakening around 7:00 A.M., fully an hour after sunrise, then a day of feeding, resting, and feeding some more. For the youngsters there were games and daring stunts to try in the forest gymnasium.

For the newborn Kongo life meant the warmth and security of his mother. She was a good mother, caring for him and protecting him at all times. During the baby's first month of life she held him close to her constantly. Even when his tiny hands grew strong enough to cling to her fur, she held him tight.

When Kongo was one month old his eyes began to lose the vacant stare they had held since he first opened them on the world. The infant's eyes began to focus on faraway objects. Within a few days his eyes followed the movements of the other gorillas. His brown eyes sparkled with curiosity, and the skinny little ape looked for all the world as if he couldn't wait to grow big enough to join in the fun.

Now the baby developed quickly. For several months he would still look small and scrawny, but he was beginning to master the gorilla way of life. When he was two months old, the first few little teeth appeared in his mouth, and he began to reach out toward leaves and branches. Anything he managed to pull in promptly went into his mouth. Once in a while Kongo tried to eat a plant that tasted bad. When this happened he quickly spat out the half-chewed mouthful, shaking his head and screwing up his face.

More than once the baby's unselective hand pulled in a leaf or a piece of bark that his mother did not consider proper gorilla food. Such items were quickly pulled from his hand before they could reach his mouth.

Around the same time that Kongo's first teeth appeared his mother began to place him on the ground for a little while at a time. The infant seemed delighted with his new freedom. Slowly and shakily he would draw himself up on his hands and knees and crawl about. His mother always watched closely and snatched him up when she decided he had had enough excitement.

Now that Kongo was a little stronger, his mother began to play with him instead of hugging him close all the time. When the group rested she would lie on her back in the sun with the baby on her stomach. She loved to pat him and tickle him, and the baby never failed to kick his legs in the air. Sometimes she took hold of his hands and raised her arms high above her head, letting the infant dangle gently. Then Kongo would look from

11

side to side, and his tiny mouth would form itself into a joyful O.

For the first time too the mother began to let other gorillas in the group touch the baby. One female seemed especially happy about this. Most of the adult females in the group had babies of their own to look after, but this female was old and wrinkled. Two of the grown gorillas and one five year old in the group were her children, but now there would be no more babies for her. Still, she could remember holding an infant and often approached the new mother, trying to touch Kongo. At first the younger female had pushed her away, but now she was less nervous about her child.

At least once a day the old gorilla approached the mother, and she turned her child over to the baby-sitter. The old female hugged Kongo and played with him. The infant gorilla quickly grew affectionate with his old aunt.

The young mother would move off a few yards, seemingly intent on searching for especially tasty food. But if the baby whimpered, she was back at the old female's side in an instant, ready to reclaim her child.

When Kongo was three months old his mother no longer allowed him to travel clinging to the hair on her stomach. When the group moved she boosted the little gorilla onto her shoulders and carried him piggyback. This way she

13

could move much more quickly. As for the little gorilla, he loved the new freedom his perch gave him to observe his surroundings as the group moved through the forest. He could walk by himself now, but he could not move fast enough to keep up with the group. He still needed his mother for traveling.

Kongo liked watching the other gorillas even better than he liked watching the forest go by from atop his mother's back. His interest in the other animals was an important part of his development. By watching the other gorillas he was learning how to be a gorilla himself.

He often imitated what he saw. From time to time most of the adult gorillas beat their chests. They did this when they were frightened or trying to scare off an intruder. Sometimes they beat their chests from happy excitement. When he was barely four months old, little Kongo began to experiment with chest-beating. For a few shaky seconds he stood up on his tiny bowed legs and thumped his open hands against his chest. The sound it made was very satisfying, and the little gorilla often practiced chest-beating after that.

As the months of Kongo's first year sped by, he grew more and more active. His young mother could hardly make him sit still. He was a six-month-old, ten-pound bundle of energy. Whenever he could struggle free of his mother, he would race off to swing on a vine, turn somersaults, or go tumbling down a hillside. Sometimes all he wanted to do was lie on his back and wave his arms and legs in the air.

Many times in his playing Kongo would roll into one of the adults. Or, when he felt very daring, he would slap a resting gorilla on the back or arm. Once he charged over to the silverback as he dozed and swatted the huge leader in the face.

Never was the infant punished for such actions. Adult gorillas seem to be exceptionally fond of children in the group. They remain tolerant of all kinds of youthful misbehavior. Even the great, dignified silverback only turned his head when the mischievous infant slapped his face.

One adult in the group was more than tolerant of Kongo's youthful exuberance. This was his old aunt. She seemed pleased when he singled her out for attention —even the roughest possible attention. Sometimes she played a trick on the baby. She would pretend to be asleep, then suddenly grab the little gorilla's leg as he tore past her. Kongo quickly caught on to the trick, but he liked the game. He continued to let his aunt trip him. The game always ended with the baby throwing his arms around the old female's neck in an affectionate hug. Then he raced off to continue his play.

15

Kongo did not always play alone. In the group he had a number of playmates close to his age. Most often he played with a baby who was two months older than he was and therefore slightly bigger and stronger. Their favorite game was fake fighting.

Late one morning Kongo sat quietly for once, allowing his old aunt to hold him and rock him. Sometimes he felt good just being a baby. Suddenly his young friend rushed up, tugged on the old female's leg, and ran off. In a flash Kongo forgot the joys of playing baby and jumped after his friend. Catching up with him, he pounced. The two gorillas rolled over and over. Both tried to seem strong and fierce, pretending to bite each other's shoulders. Finally the larger infant pinned Kongo, but a few seconds later little Kongo broke free. He stood up and beat his chest. Then he pounced again.

A three year old, bigger and stronger than the two infants put together, wandered over and decided to join the battle. Now the two former opponents joined together against the common enemy. The three began to wrestle. But the two infants at once proved too much for the larger animal, who ran off. Tired but victorious, the two little gorillas returned happily to their mothers.

Soon enough Kongo was one year old. Gorillas don't know about counting dates and ages, so his birthday

17

passed like any other day in playing, eating, and sleeping. He had come a long way in one year, from a tiny, helpless four-pound newborn to a clever, playful eighteen-pound child.

But the little gorilla had a long way to go before he would be grown up. He still spent most of his time with his mother and depended on her for much of his food, transportation, a place to sleep at night, and love.

Kumba

YEAR ONE

Nearly halfway around the world from the mountain forests of Central Africa, in the same summer of Kongo's birth, another gorilla was born. This time many people heard about the newborn gorilla because the story was broadcast on television and radio and written in newspapers. For this baby gorilla was born in the Lincoln Park Zoo, in Chicago, Illinois, U.S.A. The baby made history.

She was the first gorilla ever born in Chicago and only the fifteenth born in captivity anywhere in the world. The people at Lincoln Park named the new baby Kumba, which is also the name of a town in West Africa.

But Kumba's story really begins more than eight years earlier when a one-year-old female lowland gorilla named Mumbi arrived at Lincoln Park. Mumbi had been born in the wild, in the Cameroons in West Africa.

In the Lincoln Park Children's Zoo there is a nursery for baby animals who need special treatment. Volunteers and members of the zoo staff care for orphans, babies whose mothers reject them, and sick or hurt babies. Mumbi was placed in the nursery, where her sweet, lovable personality soon won her many friends. She got along well with humans, but she still liked to be with other apes. The nursery had no other young gorillas at that time, so Mumbi's closest ape friends were a chimpanzee named Wes and an orangutan named Jane. Mumbi lived in the Children's Zoo for about a year. Then she was moved to the Primate House.

About the same time, a young male lowland gorilla near Mumbi's age arrived at Lincoln Park. Kisoro had also been born in West Africa. Little Kisoro did not spend much time in the Children's Zoo. He stayed only long enough for the zoo staff to be sure that he was strong and healthy. Within a few weeks he was moved to the

Primate House and placed in the same cage as Mumbi.

Mumbi and Kisoro adjusted easily to life in a zoo cage. If the little apes had any memories of their earliest months in the wild, they never let their human keepers know. They did not seem to miss the African forests.

Instead of tree limbs and green vines to play on, Mumbi and Kisoro had metal bars and shelves, hanging chains, and old tires. Instead of a whole group of gorillas to play with, Mumbi and Kisoro had only each other. The zoo had no cages big enough to hold a whole group of gorillas. The animals lived by themselves or in pairs. But Mumbi and Kisoro didn't seem to mind the arrangement. They grew up happy and healthy.

In March of 1970 the zoo staff noticed a change in Mumbi. Her behavior seemed normal—she remained playful and friendly—but her belly seemed to be growing. Mumbi was pregnant.

The zoo keepers were very excited about the coming gorilla birth, but they had one problem. They didn't know when it would be. They knew that gorilla pregnancies normally last about eight and a half months, but no one had seen Mumbi and Kisoro mate. They could not be sure when the pregnancy began.

The only thing to do was keep a close watch on Mumbi to make sure that her doctor would be there

21

when the baby was born. Mumbi was going to be a mother for the first time, and like many first-time mothers she might not know how to handle her newborn baby. And Mumbi had spent most of her life in a zoo, where she had had no chance to see other gorilla mothers and babies. The Lincoln Park staff had to make sure that Chicago's first-born gorilla would survive.

The zoo keepers had no cause for worry. At about 6:00 P.M. on July 22 Mumbi's baby was born. The doctors estimated that the tiny female weighed three and a quarter pounds. Mumbi picked up the baby right away. She seemed to know what to do. Expertly she held the infant and licked it clean. She handled her baby gently, and the zoo keepers were convinced that Mumbi would not hurt her child purposely.

In order to make sure that Mumbi would feed her baby, two members of the zoo staff stayed in the Primate House watching her. Through the night Mumbi held her baby tenderly. The baby lay on its back with Mumbi supporting it with her arm or thigh. Sometimes Mumbi sat quietly looking at the baby. When she moved around the cage hand over hand on the bars overhead, she drew her legs close to her chest to keep the baby from falling. The baby clung tight with hands and feet to Mumbi's fur, but could not yet hold up its head.

Within a few days the zoo keepers were certain that

22

little Kumba was being fed properly. Mumbi seemed to have enough milk to feed her baby and appeared to be an ideal mother. Dr. Lester Fisher, the zoo's director, decided that there was nothing to worry about. Kumba would not have to be taken from her mother and raised by humans. A week after the birth the Primate House was reopened to visitors, and people met Chicago's first native-born gorilla.

For the first few weeks of Kumba's life everything was fine. Many people came to watch the new mother and baby, but Mumbi was not bothered by them. She seemed content to spend her time caring for Kumba.

Then Mumbi's behavior changed. Sometimes she ignored her baby. Sometimes she played roughly with Kumba, treating the infant like a rubber doll instead of a living gorilla. Some of the zoo keepers thought Mumbi was bored. She had always been a lively, playful animal and had always had Kisoro to play with. But Mumbi and Kisoro had been separated to make sure the father would not hurt the baby either accidentally or on purpose. Kumba herself was far too small and too weak to be a good playmate, but that no longer seemed to matter to Mumbi.

The zoo keepers could only hope that Mumbi would continue to care for her baby. In a few months Kumba would be an alert and playful baby, and there would be many lessons for Mumbi to teach her. Then perhaps Mumbi would not be bored with the child.

When Kumba was thirty-eight days old one of the members of the zoo staff saw Mumbi dragging the baby around the cage. With every step Mumbi took, Kumba bounced along the hard floor. Quickly he ran to Dr. Fisher. The zoo director realized that he would have to do what no one had wanted to do. He decided that Kumba must be taken from her mother if she was to survive.

The zoo keepers watched Mumbi closely, waiting for her to put the baby down. Even though she had been neglecting her child, they knew she would be upset if Kumba was taken from her arms. If there was a struggle, the baby might be hurt.

After a while Mumbi set the infant on the floor of the cage. The zoo keepers were ready. Mumbi was forced into an empty cage next door, and little Kumba was removed from her mother's cage.

When Mumbi saw what was happening, she started to scream. She rattled the bars of her cage. She seemed to be demanding the return of her child. But in a few minutes, after Kumba was out of her sight, Mumbi calmed down. Soon she seemed to forget about the baby. Mumbi was a happy, friendly gorilla once again.

25

The next time a gorilla was born at Lincoln Park Zoo an adult male gorilla was permitted to live in the same cage with the mother and baby. This time the mother gorilla continued to behave perfectly toward her child and was able to raise the baby herself. The zoo staff decided that when Mumbi had another baby she would also be allowed adult gorilla company. They hoped that someday she would be able to bring up her second child without human help.

As for Kumba, she was taken to the Children's Zoo nursery. Soon after her arrival in her new home she was fed milk from a baby bottle. The keepers had been worried that Kumba might not eat once she left her mother, but the tiny gorilla took the first bottle hungrily. Mumbi had not been feeding her baby properly in the last few days.

The eighteen zoo volunteers who took turns caring for Kumba fell in love with her at once. The baby gorilla was so sweet, so helpless, so loving. In many ways she seemed like a human baby. True she was a little too hairy to be human, and she did seem to have four hands instead of two hands and two feet, but these were small differences. It was hard to remember that Kumba was a gorilla.

And so the volunteers began to treat Kumba much as they would have treated a human baby. In some ways this made sense. Baby gorillas *are* very much like baby humans. They have many of the same needs. In some ways grown-up gorillas are like grown-up people. But the differences are very great too. The humans who took care of Kumba could not teach her how to be a gorilla. Only other gorillas could do that.

Like all human babies Kumba wore a diaper. Almost from the beginning she was interested in this strange piece of clothing. Well before she was a year old she learned to take her diaper off and use it as a toy. Sometimes she put it on her head to show off and attract attention. The volunteers found that Kumba often had to be rediapered a dozen times a day.

Kumba had been in the nursery only a few days when her foster mothers noticed that she was becoming crabby and irritable. She cried often and chewed on her hand. She seemed to feel better when the nipple from her bottle was rubbed against her gums. Kumba was teething. By the time she was six weeks old she had two teeth. When she was nine weeks old, four teeth showed when she opened her mouth.

At about the same time her foster mothers started to feed her cereal along with her milk. Soon after, she began to eat baby food too. She was fed a number of different kinds of food, including strained meats. Unlike gorillas in the wild, who never eat meat, most gorillas

27

who are raised in zoos seem to enjoy eating meat.

At about the age of five months Kumba began to eat some grown-up gorilla foods, like fresh fruit. Her favorites were grapes and bananas. Even better than fruit was her special Sunday morning treat of coffeecake. She had her dislikes too. She always seemed upset when she was offered liver.

Kumba was a fussy eater. Some days she would sit quietly while a volunteer spooned baby food into her mouth or handed her grapes one by one. Other days she squirmed and fidgeted, so that more food ended up outside her than inside her.

The volunteers bathed Kumba from time to time just as they would have bathed a human baby. Kumba seemed to enjoy her baths and often inspected the water with her fingers. A pan filled with water became a toy for her too. She loved to splash in the water and watch it spill over the edges.

Kumba seemed to enjoy almost anything that allowed her to be touched by her foster mothers. She sat quietly and happily while she was being brushed. She was also ticklish. When someone tickled her she rolled around on the floor, laughing until she lost her breath.

Most of Kumba's foster mothers could not bring themselves to punish her even when she deserved it. Only a few would slap her lightly when she played with her

29

food or when she chewed her diaper. But a light slap almost always made her behave—for a while anyway.

Kumba was a friendly baby, but she liked some people more than others. Her feelings for a person did not depend on whether that person punished her. In fact, some of her favorite people were those who permitted no nonsense. If Kumba liked you she would reach for your hand and lick it. She often did this with the many children who came to see her.

By the time Kumba was one year old she had become a sweet and trusting, but stubborn and spoiled child. She did exactly as she pleased and often refused to do things for herself. She preferred to cling tightly to a foster mother and act like a big baby.

She was a beautiful, healthy little gorilla. Her fur was thick and black everywhere except on the top of her head. There it was red. People who had known Mumbi when she was a baby said that Kumba looked just like her mother. But beautiful as she was, Kumba did not act like a normal one-year-old gorilla. There were many things she could not or would not do. Without a gorilla mother to teach her, Kumba had to figure out normal gorilla behavior for herself if she was going to learn it at all. She had not tried to stand up until she was five months old, and at six months she was not a good walker. Even at the age of one year she preferred being carried to walking on her own.

On Kumba's first birthday the zoo gave her a birthday party. Reporters and photographers from Chicago's newspapers were there. The members of the press were invited to take part in a contest to guess Kumba's weight. None of the newspapermen had ever weighed a baby gorilla, and all of the guesses were too high. When Kumba was placed on the scale the reporters discovered that she weighed twenty-three and a half pounds.

Kumba received many presents, including a birthday cake with her name on it. More than two hundred people came to the party. All of Chicago wished Kumba a happy birthday.

Kongo
YEAR TWO

In the mountain forest of Central Africa Kongo was playing with three friends. Now that he was fifteen months old he often played in groups. On this particular late afternoon the four youngsters had chosen a huge tree with a gently sloping trunk as their playground. The old tree was covered with slippery moss, so it made a wonderful slide.

The gorillas' basic tree game was follow-the-leader. They were all excellent climbers, and one after the other they would scramble up the tree. Then the line of young gorillas would come sliding down the trunk. At the start of the game the animals seemed pleased enough with simple feetfirst slides on their backs. Later, one of them thought of trying it headfirst on his stomach. The others thought this was fun, and it became the preferred method for a number of slides. As the game went on, the youngsters experimented with complicated side-slides and other creative variations. Each one tried to outdo the others in cleverness and daring.

Meanwhile the adult gorillas sat quietly in the gathering darkness. An old female yawned. Three adults sat near a berry bush and ate slowly, picking the berries daintily one by one. They waited for the silverback to begin building his nest. Then all would prepare for sleep. But the enormous gorilla just sat, as still as a statue.

A large female arose sleepily from a clump of bushes. She knuckle-walked over to the mossy tree where the four youngsters still played enthusiastically. She had come to claim her own child and to let the others know that it was time to stop the foolishness and get ready for bed.

The young gorillas knew immediately what she had in mind. As she stood watching them, not making a noise, the game stopped. Four pairs of brown eyes peered out at

33

the female. The children knew they would have to go to bed, but they were not about to do it docilely. The first youngster made his move. He leaped out at the female, barreling into her side. Before she could turn and grab him he scampered away, back to his own mother.

The other three children found equally interesting ways of retiring from the game and returning home. Kongo tore out from behind the tree trunk and pushed his way under the female. He ran between her legs almost toppling her over. He kept running all the way back to his mother.

1812417

The mother saw her child coming and stretched out her arms toward him. Without slowing down, Kongo reached her and threw his arms around her neck. Her arms tightened around his back, and mother and son clung to each other for several seconds.

Suddenly the little gorilla started to squirm and wriggle. His mother's arms held him even tighter. He struggled some more. Finally he broke free. But no sooner was he free than he began to dance around, making faces and waving his arms. He made soft little cries, demanding to be picked up again.

His mother pretended to ignore him. This was a game the two had played before and would play again. Someday Kongo would not need his mother. Someday he would ask to be picked up, and she would refuse him.

But for now it was still a game, and in a little while she gave in and hugged the child close again.

As the two gorillas sat quietly in the damp forest, a six-month-old baby wandered over. She tugged on the female's fur, asking to be picked up. The mother gathered the baby into her arms. For several minutes she sat cuddling the two infants. Then the smaller baby stirred, asking to be put down. Quickly she returned to her own mother.

When the silverback finally decided it was bedtime, he did not even bother to change his position. He reached out and pulled a nearby branch toward him. Within five minutes he had pulled in and crushed enough plants to make a nest rim around his body. He rose from the spot only to make sure that the nest wall was unbroken. When he was satisfied, the great gorilla curled up inside it and promptly fell asleep.

Most of the other adult gorillas were anxious to be in bed too. As soon as the silverback started making his nest, their own nest-building began. The young mother prepared a bed for herself and her child. While she was busy, Kongo wandered over to a small shrub. He climbed until he found a suitable V. Looking around, he selected a branch and pulled it toward him until it snapped. He pushed the branch beneath his feet and stamped on it until it broke into small pieces. The little gorilla repeated these actions with several other branches.

Within fifteen minutes he had constructed his first nest. Anyone could have seen how crude and unstable the platform was, but Kongo seemed pleased with his accomplishment. He sat down and looked around at the other gorillas. Most of the nests were finished. Many animals were already asleep. Kongo looked down at his mother in her nest. Darkness was falling and he could barely see her in the fading light. He needed only a few seconds to make up his mind. Abandoning his masterpiece, the little gorilla raced back to his mother and crawled into the nest.

In the months to come Kongo would build hundreds of practice nests. His technique would improve and his nest-building time would decrease. By the time he was ready to sleep alone he would be a nest-building expert.

Now that Kongo was well over a year old, he was an expert at finding his own food in the forest. His mother still kept an eye on him to make sure that interesting fuzzy caterpillars and other playthings did not become part of his diet, but most of the time he was making the right food choices on his own. She really didn't have to worry.

Even though Kongo now received almost all his nourishment from grown-up food, he still took milk from his mother. Like all babies he enjoyed nursing. It made

37

him feel warm and secure and happy, and somehow took him back to a dimly remembered time when his whole world was his mother.

His mother had started to wean him just before his first birthday. Every now and then he would ask to nurse and she would gently push him away. In the beginning her denials were few and far between. If the baby was persistent she usually gave in. As time went on she refused him more, and Kongo asked less. Now, in the middle of his second year, he took milk only rarely. He came to his mother to nurse only for comfort, when a game had not gone his way, or when he fell out of a tree, or when it was dark and he felt small and scared. At those times she almost never pushed him away. Nevertheless, before his second birthday he would be completely weaned.

Even during the dry season in the Virunga Mountains there are frequent rains. Nearly every morning the gorillas awaken in a heavy mist. Often as they bed down for the night a light drizzle falls from an overcast sky. Then the gorillas huddle in their nests, trying to keep the water from as much of their fur as possible.

In October the rainy season begins. For three long months the skies remain cloudy most of the time. Perhaps once a week the sun breaks through. But soon the sky clouds over again. The forest and its inhabitants do not have time to dry out thoroughly. Nearly every day the rain falls steadily and heavily for several hours. When it stops, the plants in the forest continue to drip, drip, drip.

The gorillas did not like the rain, but they weren't very good at figuring out ways to avoid it. Often they sat out in the open, hunched over and miserable, allowing the water to run down their backs. Every rainy season several of the gorillas caught colds. Their loud coughing and sneezing could be heard through the wet, still forest. Almost every rainy season at least one animal in the group contracted pneumonia or another severe respiratory disease and died.

During the first rainy season of Kongo's life he had been a tiny baby. His mother held him tight in her arms, close to her body. The infant had been hardly aware of the rain since he so seldom got wet.

Kongo's second rainy season was different. He had grown too big for his mother's arms to keep him completely dry. When a storm began he usually stopped his playing and huddled next to his mother's chest. She would put her arms around his back, trying to protect him. As soon as the storm had passed the little gorilla would jump up, anxious to return to his games. Sometimes if the storm continued for an especially long time he grew restless with his mother and went to his aunt for shelter.

39

One afternoon toward the end of the rainy season the group sat quietly and sadly in a driving rainstorm. They seemed dazed by all the water and unwilling to move, even though most of the animals were getting very wet. When the storm had started, all the gorillas who had been sitting in trees or bushes came down to huddle on the ground. Five animals positioned themselves under a large tree out of the worst of the rain. Three more animals tried to join them. With screams and shoves the five drove them away. Instead of seeking shelter under another tree the three gorillas now chose to sit in the clearing, where the rain pounded down on them with full force. Two young animals also remained in the clearing. They sat face to face, hugging each other as the water rolled down their backs.

Kongo sat with his mother in a clump of shrubs. The bushes were soaked, and few branches stuck out over the gorillas' heads. In truth, the two were not much better protected than the animals who had chosen to remain in the clearing.

After two hours of steady rainfall the restless little gorilla could remain in one place no longer. Leaving his mother, he knuckle-walked toward his aunt, who was sitting alone at the far side of the clearing.

The old female's body was racked by loud coughs. She was very sick. She had caught cold at the beginning

of the rainy season, and her old body was too worn out to fight the disease. In two and a half months of steady rains her soft coughs had gradually become great loud hacking noises that shook her entire body. In her weakened state she had fallen victim to an intestinal virus. She had eaten almost nothing for several days, and this had weakened her further. The old gorilla seemed to sense that she would not survive the rainy season.

When Kongo reached the old female, she did not open her arms to him as usual. She did not even look up. The child was puzzled. He tugged on her fur. Without raising her head, she pushed him. Kongo pulled again at her arm. The old gorilla coughed and pushed him as hard as she could. He fell over backward. More confused and upset, he rose and tried to push his way into the female's arms. With great effort she stood up, and still coughing, turned to walk into the forest. The little gorilla followed, easily catching up with her. Again the old female pushed him away. He began to make loud cries of distress.

Kongo's mother heard the cries. Although gorillas dislike moving in a rainstorm, she hurried toward her child. She soon found him, now desperately trying to make his aunt pay attention to him. She gathered the child up into her arms and held him until he stopped screaming. She put her son down and looked at the old female, who stood there, coughing. Walking over to her, the mother reached out and patted her on the shoulder. Then she went to her child, boosted him on her back, and returned to the group in the clearing. Still coughing, the old female walked deeper into the forest, to die alone.

During his second year Kongo continued to learn a great deal by watching the adults in the group. Whenever he was excited he would stand confidently on two feet and thump his cupped hands against his chest. He seemed to be saying, "Look at me! See how strong and clever I am!" Sometimes he thumped on other parts of his body. He lay on his back with his legs stretched out above him and drummed on the soles of his feet.

But standing up and beating on his chest was the grown-up way of showing how excited he was. In his second year Kongo added other grown-up features to the chest-beating display. Sometimes before he stood up he picked one leaf from a nearby bush and placed it between his lips. Then later he broke up a round of chest-beating by ripping great handfuls of leaves and branches from the bushes and throwing them into the air. Just like the adult male animals, the little gorilla liked to end his chest-beating displays by throwing more vegetation about.

When Kongo reached his second birthday, he weighed thirty-five pounds. His movements were no

43

longer shaky, but quick and confident. He found all his own food now and did not take milk from his mother. Yet in many ways he was still an infant. He still slept with his mother every night. He still rode on her back when the group traveled, for he was too little to keep up with the group on his own. And he still needed his mother's love and comfort.

Kumba

YEAR TWO

Kumba was big for her age. The good food and loving care she received in the nursery had kept her strong and healthy. As she moved into her second year, she acted like a playful, slightly shy, slightly spoiled human baby. Most of the time she didn't behave like a gorilla at all. She did know how to knuckle-walk, but most often she preferred not to walk at all. She had a heavy chain hanging from the top of her private cage, but she had not yet learned to swing on it. True, she sometimes beat her chest like a wild gorilla. But some of her foster mothers thought she might have learned this by imitating people who beat their own chests at Kumba. They weren't convinced that Kumba really understood what chest-beating was all about.

For her first two weeks away from her mother Kumba had been fed and cared for by the man who ran the zoo nursery. After that her care had been turned over to women. By the time of her first birthday Kumba acted happy and secure only with her foster mothers. She did not even want a man to pick her up.

One of the zoo keepers who wanted to help care for Kumba decided to help her get over her fear of men. Every day he came to see her. He talked to her and played with her. Gradually Kumba began to relax when he was around. She recognized him as a friend. At the end of two months she hugged him. From then on she loved to have him hold her and carry her around. Kumba was still shy with men she didn't know, but she was no longer afraid.

Like human babies Kumba had regular medical check-ups. She never minded as long as she thought the doctor was just playing with her. She liked to inspect the doctor and all his medical instruments. So many of them made good toys. So much of the examination seemed like a game. And she got so much attention!

The trouble came when the doctor got around to the serious business of checking on Kumba's health. She hated having the cold stethoscope against her chest, so she rarely sat quietly long enough for the doctor to check her heartbeat.

It was even worse when she needed an injection. Gorillas are susceptible to many of the same diseases as humans, including some very serious illnesses like polio. Most apes who grow up in zoos receive the same vaccines as human children. But Kumba didn't know that shots were good for her. Like human children of her age she knew only that it hurt to be stuck with a needle. Each time it happened she screamed and bared her teeth. She tried hard to scare the doctor away. Of course it never worked, and Kumba received all the injections and all the examinations she needed. After each of the doctor's visits she was given a special treat to eat, even if she hadn't really been very good.

In spite of excellent medical care, Kumba did get sick once in a while. Sometimes she ate too much or too fast. Then an upset stomach would make her unhappy and crabby for a while. Like all gorillas, Kumba caught cold easily. Her foster mothers knew that respiratory diseases can be very serious in gorillas, so they were alert

47

for any signs of illness in Kumba. If she began to cough or sneeze or developed a runny nose, her temperature was checked at once. If she was running a fever, she was given cold medicine and extra vitamins until everything was back to normal. All in all Chicago's first native-born gorilla was one of the healthiest babies in the city.

Kumba loved to play, and she never lacked for toys. When she was very young, a mobile of brightly colored plastic shapes had been hung from the top of her cage. At first she had only watched it. Then she began to reach for it with her hands and feet. The mobile was raised so that she would not tear it apart. Soon it had to be raised again. Finally it could be raised no higher. By climbing and jumping, Kumba could still reach it. The mobile was removed. Much stronger than a human child of her own age, Kumba was ready for sturdier toys.

One new toy she received was a present from a toy company. The toy was supposed to be indestructible. The people from the company thought they would have a terrific advertisement if they could say, "Kumba loves this toy. Our toy is so strong that even a gorilla can't break it." They hoped that many human parents would be so impressed that they would buy the toy for their own children.

Kumba did like the new toy. She liked it so much

that she played with it all the time. Within a week the toy was in three pieces instead of one. Now there could be no advertisement about the indestructible toy. This didn't matter a bit to Kumba. She simply had three new toys.

Kumba enjoyed playing most when she had company. It was more fun playing with someone than playing alone. Since she had spent nearly all her life so far with humans, it was not surprising that she thought people were better playmates than animals. With people who thought she was the cutest thing they had ever seen, Kumba could be the center of attention. Most of the time she could get her own way. She trusted people and knew they wouldn't hurt her.

Kumba's foster mothers thought that she should have some animal playmates too. Unfortunately, though, there were no other little gorillas in the nursery. When Kumba was nine months old another baby gorilla had been born in the Lincoln Park Zoo. But Benga, as the new baby was called, had been cared for by her mother and was living in the Primate House. Benga could not be Kumba's playmate.

Even though she was the only gorilla, Kumba was not the only ape in the zoo nursery. There were also young chimpanzees and a baby orangutan. The other apes seemed perfectly happy to be Kumba's friends, but Kumba would have nothing to do with them. Each time anyone tried to introduce her to a chimp, Kumba would cling tightly to her foster mother. If the animals were left together, she huddled miserably in a corner until either she or the chimp was removed.

Well, Kumba was just shy, thought her foster mothers. Maybe the chimps were too eager. Maybe their constant antics frightened the slower, quieter gorilla. Maybe Kumba would do better with an orangutan, who also was slow moving and quiet compared to the chimps. But they discovered that Kumba was afraid of orangutans too.

It began to look as if Kumba's friends would all be humans. As it turned out, though, there were some animals that Kumba liked a lot—cats.

The Lincoln Park Zoo has a large collection of big cats. Many lions, tigers, black leopards, snow leopards, jaguars, and cougars have been born there. Often there are one or more kittens in the nursery, either because the mother is unable to care for them or because they are recovering from an illness or injury.

Kumba liked all the kittens she met, but her favorites were the little tigers, the biggest, calmest, and slowest of the cats. Kumba seemed to feel most at ease with them. Her special favorite was a tiger cub named Tara.

Tara was a Siberian tiger. Siberians are the largest of the tigers and they are an endangered species, close to extinction in the wild. When a Siberian tiger is born in a

zoo, it is a special event, and the baby is treated royally. Tara was no exception. The two special babies, Kumba the gorilla and Tara the Siberian tiger, quickly became friends.

A baby tiger and a baby gorilla playing happily together was a strange sight, one that brought visitors back to Lincoln Park again and again. Kumba and Tara wrestled, chased each other, and fought with mock ferocity. Kumba pulled gently on Tara's tail. Sometimes she straddled Tara's back and walked along over her on two feet as the tiger padded about on four.

Chicago's weather in winter is too cold and snowy for gorillas to go outside. But on warm days in the spring and fall, and nearly every day in the summertime, Kumba was taken outdoors. Often, especially when she was taken into the playground—a cement area filled with toys and interesting things to climb on—Kumba clung to her foster mother. She turned shyly away from the many visitors who came to see her.

She was happier when she was allowed to play on the green lawn. There Kumba didn't need man-made playthings. There she seemed most like a normal, playful gorilla child. She inspected the grass with her fingers, her nose, and her tongue. She picked up twigs and poked around in the dirt. She patiently searched through the grass for the round white flowers of clover plants. When she discovered one, she daintily picked the flower and popped it into her mouth.

Kumba loved the outdoors, and in time she grew more daring in her games. After many trips outside she no longer needed the security of a foster mother next to her. She learned to go off on her own to play. She invented a game with the nursery doors which seemed to please her no matter how often she played it. The nursery had two doors leading to the outside, one right next to the other. One door was an entrance, the other an exit. Kumba learned to dash out the exit door, make a quick run in front of the building, and dash back in through the entrance door. Without stopping to catch her breath, she would repeat the game again and again until she was caught by a keeper. Each time she played the game, she would run farther out from the building.

Another outdoor game Kumba liked was hide-and-seek. In Kumba's version of the game she was always the hider and a human was always the seeker. She quickly learned which bushes made the best hiding places. Kumba might have won the game more often, though, if she hadn't continued to make the same mistake. She loved to take her friend Tara the tiger into hiding with her. Tara seemed to catch on to the idea of the game and crouched low in the bushes. But she never managed to

53

hide her tail. Kumba's keepers could easily discover the hiding place of the tiger and the gorilla. All they had to do was look for a long striped tail sticking out from under a bush.

The time passed quickly and Kumba was two years old. She was a big girl, weighing forty-one pounds. Of course the zoo gave her another birthday party. Even though she was more comfortable with crowds than she had been a year before, Kumba was still nervous and shy in front of all the strangers who had come to celebrate her birthday. She stuck close to the people she knew well as she sampled her birthday cake with its two candles.

In Kumba's first two years of life she had been a happy, healthy baby. She had also been spoiled. She had been given nearly everything she wanted and had rarely been punished. She had been allowed to act like a helpless human infant. Kumba had no way of knowing that she was supposed to be a gorilla.

Kongo

YEAR THREE

Kongo, the little gorilla in the African mountains, was two years and three months old. It was morning, and the group was feeding. The adults moved little, intent upon their work. The youngsters, including Kongo, were not nearly as disciplined. Every few minutes a chase or a wrestling match interrupted their search for food.

Meanwhile another group of gorillas was moving

toward them through the forest. The new group contained twelve animals, among them three silverback males. In this group, as in all gorilla groups with more than one silverback, one of the huge males was the undisputed leader. Another was second-in-command. Yet the leader did not keep his position by terrorizing the second and third males. The two assistant silverbacks appeared to respect his leadership and follow him willingly. They did not try to take over. For his part the leader seemed pleased to have the companionship of the other two males as well as their help in protecting the group.

Originally this group's home range had been on the lower slopes of the mountain. They had never encountered Kongo's group, which preferred the higher, more isolated slopes. But now the new group was being forced from its territory. Some African farmers, whose village was located nearby, had decided to clear more of the mountain land for farming. Each day the men came into the forest with knives and fire to cut and burn the wild vegetation. Each day the silverback moved his group a little farther up the slope away from the men.

The gorillas were reluctant to leave their home range. Going into a new area made them nervous, but it was dangerous to remain too close to men. Sometimes groups of gorillas had raided African farms, tearing up sweet potato plants and destroying banana trees. Then

57

the farmers had attacked them with clubs and spears, killing many animals. Now the gorillas were protected by national laws. Still, the farmers in remote areas sometimes tracked them with dogs and killed them for sport.

Big as they were, the gorillas never fought back. They did try to scare the men away by roaring and beating their chests. But if this did not work, the gorillas ran away. When cornered, they fell to the ground, hiding their heads. There was no doubt that the silverback was right to lead his group away from the men.

For five days the group retreated. They followed no definite path, winding their way back and forth through the forest. They did not seem to hurry, but they were moving ever farther from the human settlement, ever closer to the home range of Kongo's group.

On the sixth day of their retreat the gorillas came to a river—a stream, really, since it was only about ten feet wide and a few inches deep. The animals could easily have waded through the water to the opposite bank, but they did not. Like all wild gorillas, they disliked water that ran on the ground as much as water that fell from the sky. So rather than get their feet wet, the gorillas walked along the stream until they found a place where a fallen tree formed a natural bridge. With the third-ranking silverback in the lead the twelve gorillas walked over the water. Not one was dunked or splashed.

The water problem successfully solved, the silver-back leader and his aides continued to move the group slowly but steadily up the mountain. Within a week they had moved deep into the home range of Kongo's group. One night the two groups nested less than half a mile apart.

The next morning Kongo was busy swinging on a vine when the silverback leader of his group noticed the intruders. The huge male looked up, a mouthful of Galium vine dangling from his lips, and stared. Ever so slowly he continued to chew, and the greenery disappeared bit by bit between the moving jaws. The silverback was a relaxed sort of leader. He wanted to know what was going on, but at this point the new gorillas didn't appear to be anything to get excited about.

The silverback leader of the new group was also a calm, easygoing type, but his second-in-command was more excitable. When the second silverback noticed they were not alone in the forest, he sat up straight and tall and tilted his head so that his chin pointed toward the sky. He began to make a low hooting sound.

The hoots continued, growing louder and faster all the time. Suddenly the silverback stopped hooting and picked one leaf from a handy bush. This he placed between his lips. Still sitting up straight, he looked around

menacingly. The other gorillas in his group moved off to a safe distance and watched. He began to hoot again and the leaf fell from his mouth.

The hoots grew louder and faster. Soon they were so fast and so loud that they seemed to make one continuous roar. The silverback stood up, tore great handfuls of leaves and branches from the shrubs, and tossed them in the air. He began to beat his chest and run toward Kongo's group, hooting all the while. He dropped to all fours. He crashed through the bushes, hitting out at anything in his path. The silverback stopped only a few yards from Kongo on his rope vine. There he thumped the ground hard with his hand.

All the gorillas of both groups had watched the display with interest. None was really frightened. There was no reason to be. They had seen such displays before and knew that the only danger lay in staying in the chest-beater's path. They knew that the ground-thumping signaled the display's end. Sure enough, the second silverback now sat quietly.

The great display over, the gorillas of the second group settled down to feed calmly. The animals of the two groups were strangers, but none had reason to be afraid. Gorillas may become involved in small squabbles, but they never fight seriously. Here on the mountain slope there was enough food for all. The new gorillas would be permitted to stay just as long as they wanted.

Even so, the adult animals remained shy and cautious. They watched the new group with interest but did not dare to make friends. The younger animals were more outgoing. For several minutes Kongo watched a youngster about his own age in the new group. The newcomer was playing a fascinating game. He had pulled up a clump of moss from the forest floor and was now balancing it on his forehead. He seemed proud of himself as he walked slowly about on two legs, eyes pointed toward the sky.

With his head in this position the youngster did not see Kongo racing toward him. Kongo took a flying leap at the newcomer, tackling him around the legs and sending both animals sprawling. Eight limbs tangled and untangled then tangled again as the two gorillas wrestled. In the first attack the clump of moss had been launched into the air. For a time it lay forgotten at the base of a bush.

Only when the combatants lay quietly, exhausted from their wrestling match, did they remember the clump of moss. In a renewed burst of energy they dashed off to reclaim this prize. The newcomer reached it first. He placed it once again on his forehead and paraded about, showing off for his new friend.

Kongo had to try this wonderful game. He reached out and snatched the moss from his friend's face. He

placed it on top of his head and walked around to show that he was not about to be outdone. The newcomer dashed up and stole the moss. But his getaway wasn't quick enough. Each animal held one end of the prized clump, and a mighty tug of war followed. The contest had hardly begun when the clump split in the middle, sending each gorilla spilling over backward with half the moss.

The problem was solved. Each gorilla now had his own toy, and the two played happily together for almost half an hour.

The feeding period was ending for Kongo's group. The silverback had decided it was time to move on. Kongo's mother walked over to let her child know it was time to climb onto her back and travel. But the little gorilla was not ready to leave. He was having too much fun playing a new game with a new friend. He pretended he did not know his mother was there.

His mother waited patiently as long as she could. Then she saw that the other gorillas in the group were starting to move off. She walked over to her son and picked him up. Kongo immediately began to scream and wave his arms. He was now quite large and very determined not to be held. Breaking free of his mother, he jumped up and down, then rolled on the ground, screaming all the while. He was most upset and intent on getting his own way. If he wanted to play, he would play.

His mother turned and began to walk slowly away, following the departing group. For a few seconds Kongo looked triumphant. Then all of a sudden his expression changed. His mother was disappearing! Forgetting his friend and the moss-balancing game, he tore after his mother. The little gorilla leaped onto her shoulders. Mother and son followed the group into the forest.

In the next few weeks the new group of gorillas remained in the same range. The two groups met many times and often fed or nested together. Kongo had many chances to play with his new friend. Sometimes when it rained he did not return to his mother but sat hugging his playmate to keep dry.

These weeks were especially happy ones for Kongo. Not only did he enjoy the company of his new friend, but he was also growing bigger and stronger. He was growing too large for his mother to carry him comfortably on her back and too strong to need to be carried. By the time he was two and a half years old the little gorilla could keep up with the group by himself.

Finally, for some reason of his own, the silverback leader of the new group decided it was time to move on. Just as he had gradually led his group into the home range of Kongo's group, so he gradually led the gorillas out. The two groups met less and less, and then one day the new group was gone. The gorillas had moved to the other side of the mountain.

Although his new friend had gone away, Kongo remembered their games together. And he had many playmates in his own group. Within a short time all the young gorillas in the group knew about the moss-balancing game, and it quickly became a favorite.

For six months after he could travel by himself, Kongo continued to sleep in his mother's nest at night. Then one evening just before his third birthday he built a perfect nest in a small tree. After much practice the little gorilla had become an expert and he had completed the nest in five minutes' time. As he sat in the finished nest Kongo looked around. His eyes found his mother, settling down in a shrub nest not far away. The light faded and still the little gorilla sat. As darkness fell he curled up and went to sleep.

After this Kongo built his own nest nearly every night. Sometimes he would awaken a few hours before dawn, leave his nest, and spend the rest of the night with his mother. Sometimes he would fall asleep in his own nest and not wake until morning. Then, when the first rays of the sun hit him, he would leave his nest, run to his mother, and hug her.

Kongo was now three years old. He was no longer an infant. He weighed sixty pounds. He no longer needed his mother to survive. He could get his own food, keep pace with a moving group, and build his own nest for sleeping. Still, he spent much time with his mother, not out of need but out of affection.

The young mother was pregnant again. Before her first child reached the age of four, her second baby would be born. Even then she would continue to enjoy Kongo's company. She would let him play with the baby before she allowed any other gorillas to touch it. As long as she lived, Kongo would be special to her.

In the years to come Kongo would continue to grow in size and strength. By the time of his fifth birthday he would weigh about a hundred and twenty pounds. By the time he reached six he would no longer be called a juvenile but a young adult. He would play less and take on the more serious attitude of a grown-up gorilla. And yet he would still have more growing to do. He might weigh two hundred pounds by the age of eight. And still he would grow, taking on the weight and appearance of an adult male gorilla. Between the ages of six and ten he would be a blackback. Then, when he had his full growth and weighed close to four hundred pounds, twice as much as a fully grown female, the black fur on his back would start to turn silver. This happens only to male gorillas.

67

By the time Kongo reached twelve, the young silverback might even be the leader of the group.

Kongo would make a good leader when the time came. His years of living with his mother as part of the group had taught him how to survive. If men did not interfere—if they did not take more of the gorillas' territory each year—and if he remained strong and healthy Kongo could look forward to as much as thirty more happy years of life in the African mountains.

Kumba

YEAR THREE

In the warm summer and early fall following Kumba's second birthday the famous gorilla's life changed little. She continued to play outdoors when the weather was good. She continued to get all the love and attention any child could demand from her foster mothers. And she continued to act like a big baby whenever it suited her, which was most of the time.

But in some important ways Kumba herself was changing. For one thing, she was growing. She was becoming far too big to be picked up and carried. She was growing strong too. She could easily hurt someone by accident in a game. She could climb over the nursery's room dividers with ease. She could break almost any toy she was given. Clearly the nursery would not outlast a rapidly growing spoiled brat of a baby gorilla.

The people at Lincoln Park Zoo were worried about Kumba's social development too. There were no animals for her to play with. Tara the tiger had gone to the Lion House to live with other cats. Once again Kumba's only friends were humans. She had never known another ape.

Again Kumba was introduced to the young chimpanzees in the nursery. Again she stubbornly refused to have anything to do with them. She sat in a corner watching her human friends when the chimps tried to include her in their games. Sometimes she made a terrible fuss. She cried and screamed until her foster mothers took pity on her and took her away. The chimps seemed to realize that she was afraid of them and delighted in teasing her.

The situation was critical. If something were not done, in a few years the Lincoln Park Zoo would have on its hands one wrecked nursery, several wrecked foster mothers, and a two-hundred-pound gorilla who thought she was a human baby. If there was any hope of Kumba's growing up to be a normal ape she would have to learn to live with other gorillas right away.

So when Kumba was two years and four months old she was taken from the nursery and sent to live in the Primate House. From then on she would not be diapered and fed and picked up and cuddled like a human baby. She would be cared for by zoo keepers like all the other gorillas. Of course she would be treated with affection, but she would have much less contact with humans and far more contact with apes than ever before.

Kumba was placed in a cage next door to a six-year-old gorilla named Debbie. Between Kumba's cage and Debbie's cage there was a metal door that could be opened only by the keepers. The plan was to open the door for a little while each day to allow the two gorillas to get used to one another gradually. The keepers hoped that after a while the door could be opened for good, that the two gorillas would become friends, and that Debbie would show Kumba just what being a gorilla really meant.

Debbie had come to Lincoln Park Zoo as a baby nearly six years before. She had lived in the nursery and had been cared for by volunteers just like Kumba. But Debbie had had one big advantage. She had spent much of her time in the nursery with June, a chimpanzee about her own age who had been born at the zoo. Debbie had always been a slower moving, shier ape than June, but the little gorilla and the little chimp had seemed to enjoy each other's company. Some of the people who cared for them even claimed that Debbie was the brains of the outfit, always thinking up new tricks for June to perform.

When Debbie and June grew too large for the nursery, they were moved into the Primate House. Since the zoo wants all its animals to grow up happy and healthy and to have babies of their own, June was placed with other chimps in a big cage, while Debbie went to live in a cage next to other gorillas.

At first Debbie acted shy and unhappy in her new home. After a while, though, she began to play happily with the tire that hung from the top of her cage. She turned somersaults and swung from her cage bars. But she remained very gentle and loving with humans. She always enjoyed inspecting any new object she could get her hands on. She held things carefully, though, never throwing them or breaking them on purpose. Debbie seemed to be the perfect choice for Kumba's cagemate.

When the door between the two cages was opened for the first time, Debbie peered curiously at the new opening in the wall. She walked over to the door and stuck her head through. Crouching at the opening, half in one cage and half in the other, Debbie looked around. She saw Kumba, who was huddled miserably in a corner of her cage. Debbie walked through the door. She moved cau-

tiously toward Kumba. Slowly, ever so slowly, she reached out a finger and gently touched Kumba's shoulder. In an instant Kumba was up, screaming as if she had been attacked, just as she had done with the chimpanzees. Debbie quickly retreated to the calm of her own cage.

It didn't take long before Debbie realized that Kumba was afraid of her. Teasing Kumba then became a favorite game. When cage life became boring, Debbie could liven it up by chasing Kumba around, pretending to attack her.

Kumba probably knew that Debbie would not really hurt her. Even so, she often looked as if she were wishing for the comfortable, comforting world of the nursery. She developed a new habit. She crouched in a corner of the shelf at the back of her cage and stretched out her chest and arms along the shelf. Then she moved her arms and chest back and forth along the metal. Again and again she repeated the same motion. After a time, she had rubbed so hard and so often that she managed to wear away some of her fur.

Within a few weeks Kumba discovered that tantrums did her no good when Debbie came after her. No matter how much she screamed, her foster mothers would not rescue her. The most she could hope for was to have the door between the cages closed. And the door would always open again.

74

Kumba also discovered that if Debbie could tease, she could be teased too. More and more often Kumba turned the tables and went after Debbie. Visitors thought it was funny to watch Kumba chasing a gorilla twice her own size. Sometimes Kumba didn't seem to know when to stop. She attacked Debbie again and again until Debbie finally lost her temper, baring her teeth and barking threats at Kumba.

The keepers soon decided that Kumba and Debbie were used to each other. They hadn't exactly become the best of friends, but they did seem to have come to some sort of understanding. Neither one would really hurt the other. Debbie could scare Kumba, but Kumba could also scare Debbie. Now the door between the two cages was left open almost all the time. Even so, Kumba spent most of her days in her cage, and Debbie was happy to stay on her own side much of the time.

Over the next few months Kumba began to show signs of her old playfulness. She even started to try new games, games she had never played in the nursery. She ran and jumped around her cage. She climbed the bars on the side of the cage and swung from the bars on the top by her hands and feet. Sometimes she traveled in classic ape fashion, hand over hand, on the overhead bars. She clapped her hands and beat her chest.

75

Kumba had made much progress by the time her third birthday neared. She was getting along in her cage and had mastered new gorilla skills. She seemed to be finding out about some of the things she had missed in her early life with humans. Her keepers decided that Kumba was ready for more ape company. She and Debbie were moved into a cage with two older gorillas.

The zoo people were pleased with the new arrangement. The four gorillas seemed pleased too. Even Kumba accepted the situation. There were no tantrums. She was still shy and still seemed to like humans better than gorillas, but she had made remarkable progress.

For her third birthday Kumba again had a celebration. The little gorilla hosted a party in the Children's Zoo at which the featured guests were baby animals of other endangered species. There was even a Siberian tiger.

Kumba loved the attention she received at her party. It was not easy for her human friends to return her to the cage in the Primate House. But the zoo staff knew that Kumba's only chance for life as a normal gorilla was with other gorillas, not with humans. She had to go back.

For the most important part of her childhood Kumba had not known that she was a gorilla. She had never had the chance to learn from a whole group of gorillas. She didn't know how to survive in the African forests. Luckily for Kumba she didn't need nearly so many skills to survive in a zoo. With the expert care she received she would undoubtedly live a long and healthy life.

But the staff at Lincoln Park Zoo wanted more for Kumba. They wanted her to grow up and have babies of her own—zoo-born gorillas from a zoo-born mother. When the planned new Primate House with its jungle-like, barless cages was completed, they hoped that Lincoln Park's first native-born gorilla would be ready to live with a group of eight or ten other gorillas. People could not teach her what she needed to know. She could learn only from other gorillas. Time would tell if she would ever learn. At the time of her third birthday all the people who cared about her crossed their fingers and hoped that someday Kumba would find out just what kind of magnificent, special creature she was—a gorilla.

A WORD ABOUT
GORILLAS AND ZOOS

A lot of people feel sorry for animals in zoos. They wish that all of them could be free to roam the Central African forests like little Kongo and his group. And until recently wild gorillas probably did have much happier lives than zoo gorillas.

For a long time people did not know very much about the things gorillas needed to survive. Babies were captured in Africa for sale to zoos in Europe and America. Usually hunters captured the babies only after shooting the mothers. Many small gorillas sickened and died even before they reached the foreign zoos. Others lived only a few years.

A zoo gorilla who did live to grow up usually didn't have a happy life. Most zoos had only one gorilla who sat bored and alone in a dreary cage. Some grew fat from lack of exercise and lack of anything to do but eat. Others grew bad-tempered because they were so unhappy. The gorillas most people saw were fat or frightening or both, so people thought all gorillas were that way.

Then things began to change. In Africa the human population began to grow at an alarming rate. People needed more land for more cities, for more farms to raise more food. They began to move into gorilla territory. Many gorillas were killed or captured. Those that remained retreated into the densest parts of the jungle, far away from humans. But the shrunken jungle habitat could not support so many gorillas. As the human population of Africa grew, the gorilla population dropped. Soon there were so few left that human experts said they were an endangered species.

By the 1950s, directors of modern zoos had learned what kinds of food gorillas need to grow strong and what they like to eat. They had learned about medical care that prevented or cured gorilla diseases. They had learned that gorillas are highly intelligent animals who need something to do besides stare at zoo visitors all day. And they had learned that gorillas are social animals who need the company of other gorillas to be happy and well adjusted.

Zoo directors were worried that wild gorillas might become extinct. It would not be right to continue to capture the animals from the wild when there were so few left. If visitors were to continue to see them in zoos, then zoos would have to breed gorillas.

Someday in the not too distant future gorillas could become extinct in the wild. Perhaps if people could watch the animals living and behaving in zoos much as they did in the wild, humans would begin to think that saving the gorilla from extinction was important. Maybe they would write letters and give money to create gorilla refuges in Africa before it was too late. And if they could not save the wild gorillas, at least they could save the species in zoos.

Today the best zoos try to give their gorillas everything they need to thrive and to reproduce. This is not always easy. Suitable housing that looks like the African jungle, with good lighting and climate controls, is complicated and expensive to build and maintain. Most zoo gorillas have not grown up in normal gorilla groups, so they have not been able to learn normal gorilla behavior. It is often difficult for such animals to adjust to living together as gorillas do in the wild. And zoo people still do not know everything they would like to know about gorillas.

But many of the problems are being solved. Each year more gorilla births are recorded in zoos. In many cities people are beginning to care enough about gorillas to build them the best possible housing. At the Lincoln Park Zoo, the apes will soon have a new home. Two groups of gorillas will live in jungle settings. Human visitors will see a little of how gorillas live in the wild. And perhaps the sight of Kumba and her companions in a beautiful artificial environment will give people the determination to save the beautiful natural environment of wild gorillas like Kongo.

Alice Schick

knows Kumba, the young gorilla in Chicago's Lincoln Park Zoo, well, having been an honorary foster parent through the zoo's Adopt-an-Ape program. Ms. Schick grew up on Long Island and went to school at Northwestern University near Chicago. She now lives with her husband Joel, who is an artist, and seven cats in New York City and Massachusetts.

Joseph Cellini

is well known for his book illustrations, posters, paintings and graphic art. He is particularly interested in animal and nature subjects. Born in Budapest, Hungary, Mr. Cellini now lives in Leonia, New Jersey, with his wife, who is also a book illustrator.